ICELAND

ICELAND

THE LAND OF FIRE AND ICE

CHRIS McNAB

amber
BOOKS

First published in 2019

Copyright © 2019 Amber Books Ltd

Published by
Amber Books Ltd
United House
North Road
London
N7 9DP
United Kingdom
www.amberbooks.co.uk
Instagram: amberbooksltd
Facebook: www.facebook.com/amberbooks
Twitter: @amberbooks

Project Editor: Michael Spilling
Designer: Keren Harragan
Picture Research: Terry Forshaw, Justin Willsdon

ISBN: 978-1-78274-772-7

Printed in China

Contents

Introduction

The word 'extraordinary' is one that can be over-used in the literature of travel and exploration, especially in today's increasingly homogeneous world. But if any place could lay claim to the description, it is Iceland. Nestled in the far, frigid north of the Atlantic Ocean, balanced on the edge of the Arctic Circle, Iceland has forged its own unique way of life in a landscape literally awesome in scale, beauty and power. It is as if the natural world is constantly attempting to outdo itself in vast glaciers, rumbling and active volcanoes, bubbling geothermal pools and mudflats, black lava fields, towering basalt cliffs, thunderous waterfalls, white-foam seas – but also soft meadows and pastures and gentle harbours. It is an island that simply cannot fail to impress. Yet Iceland is as much about its history and people as its landscape. The island's small population of c. 339,000 has today fused millennia of tradition with the best of modernity, resulting in a vibrant, colourful yet stoic culture, embodied in architecture, music, art, literature, myth, religion and many other cultural phenomena. For in Iceland, people and nature cannot be separated.

ABOVE:
A picturesque evening scene across
Lake Tjörnin in Reykjavik.

OPPOSITE:
Jagged basalt rock columns form the
Reynisdrangar Sea Cliffs, Southern Iceland.

Capital Region and Southern Peninsula

For most of the thousands of visitors who flock to Iceland every year, the initial destination is the island's capital, Reykjavík. The city is a unique cultural hub nestled in the far north of the Atlantic Ocean. Its population of 123,000 souls (217,000 in Greater Reykjavík) seems to produce a disproportionate amount of art and cultural expression, including painting, literature and sculpture. This creative leaning, welded to the resilient Icelandic spirit, is evident all around the city, not least in the graffiti and murals that adorn the sides of many buildings, both official and domestic. Reykjavík also boasts fine architecture, from the colourful invitation of domestic housing, to the lofty visions of churches, cathedrals, museums and civic centres. Add food and shopping, and little wonder Reykjavík is a strengthening magnet for the world's travellers.

Yet Iceland transitions quickly from urban to nature. To the south of the capital, the Reykjanes Peninsula gives many travellers their introduction to Iceland's phenomenal coastal landscape and wildlife. The Peninsula, a UNESCO Global Geopark, is contoured by volcanoes, mountains, river-ripped valleys, steaming thermal lakes and rivers, and a jagged and moody coastline. Villages and towns dot the Peninsula, as do solitary lighthouses, throwing their beams of light out across bays and seas, warning the boats that still ply the coastal shipping lanes.

OPPOSITE:
City Hall, Reykjavík
Seeming to float upon the waters of the Tjörnin Pond in central Reykjavík, the Reykjavík City Hall was built in 1992, and houses many of the city's executive functions, including the Mayor's office; it also plays host to artistic and cultural events. In the left background we see the Landakotskirkja (Landakot's Church), formally the Basilica of Christ the King, the cathedral of the Catholic Church in Iceland.

Perlan Museum, Reykjavík
Rising 25.7m (84ft) above Reykjavík, the Perlan Museum is one of the city's most evocative landmarks, especially as seen in this view from the tower of nearby Hallgrímskirkja Church. The building was designed by Ingimundur Sveinsson and built in the late 1980s. The dome (a 1991 addition) houses a 360-degree viewing deck on the fourth floor.

Perlan Museum, Reykjavík
Form meets function at the Perlan Museum: the glass dome sits atop six vast storage tanks, five of them each with a capacity for 4 million litres (1 million gallons) of geothermal hot water, from there pumped around the city. One of the storage tanks is used for museum exhibits.

Coastline, near Reykjavík
An aerial photograph taken on the approach to Reykjavík hints at the sparsely populated nature of Iceland. The island has a population of just 339,000, and most of that is concentrated in the towns and villages scattered around the complex coastline.

Free Church, Reykjavík
The Free Church in Reykjavík (foreground) stands in traditional simplicity against the backdrop of the 73m (239ft) tall Hallgrímskirkja Lutheran Church. The Free Church was built in 1899, nearly a century prior to the consecration of the Hallgrímskirkja in 1986.

OPPOSITE:

Downtown Reykjavík
Here we have a bird's eye view of downtown Reykjavík from the observation deck of Hallgrímskirkja Church. In the distance is the Old Harbour, replete with attractions for the tourist age, including restaurants, museums and boat services for whale watching and puffin viewing.

ABOVE:

Town houses, Reykjavík
The Icelandic capital boasts an array of architectural styles. Strong colours feature heavily in domestic low-rise architecture, an expression of both traditionalism and modernism. These buildings are in Reykjavík 101, at the very heart of the city.

OPPOSITE:

Town house, Reykjavík
Many of Iceland's buildings
are timber-framed but with
outer walls of corrugated
iron. While such buildings are
found elsewhere in the world,
in Iceland the corrugations
of the iron typically run
vertically rather than
horizontally, a configuration
that allows ice and rain to
run off more effectively.

LEFT:

Red house, Reykjavík
A much-photographed red
house in central Reykjavík
shows off a traditional
architectual style to vibrant
effect. The aforementioned
corrugated iron revolution
in Icelandic housing design
began in the 19th century.
Contrasting wood-framed
windows provide an inviting,
cosy feel to the buildings.

ABOVE:

Shop, Reykjavík
With the ups and downs of
Iceland's fishing industry
since the 1990s, shopping
and tourism have become
increasingly important to
Reykjavík's cultural and
financial life. As this quaint
shop illustrates, a commercial
focus does not necessarily
lose touch with the
traditional aspects of life.

LEFT:

Old Harbour, Reykjavík
A large bank of tyres
provide a protective buffer
for ships docking against
the quayside in Reykjavík.
Although the harbour is still
a focal point for fishing, it
has become a commercial
and tourist boom area.
Some local restaurants
combine fishing and
tourism, by offering to cook
whatever offshore anglers
bring back with them.

OPPOSITE:

Drekinn, Reykjavík
The Drekinn restaurant
('Dragon' in English) is one
of many small eateries dotted
throughout Reykjavík. The
city has an ever-burgeoning
service sector, fuelled by
the exponential growth in
tourism, which shows no
signs of slowing down.

Icelandic wool

The wool from Icelandic sheep produces a very high grade of insulation in products ranging from socks to jumpers, perfect for the sub-zero winters. The fleece has two layers of wool, a long and coarse upper layer called tog, and a soft and fluffy inner layer called pel. Spun together, the resulting material is warm, tough and waterproof.

Fish and beer

Fried fish and a glass of locally brewed cold beer are two cornerstones of Icelandic cuisine. The most common seafoods eaten on the islands are haddock, Atlantic wolffish, salmon, monkfish or cod. Stockfish also remains popular – this is unsalted fish that has been air-dried on the sea foreshore.

Restaurant, Reykjavík

A speciality of Icelandic cuisine, *skata*, or fermented skate, divides opinion in the country. It has been described as having the taste of rotting fish, plus an intense smell of ammonia. The only other country that serves this dish commonly is South Korea.

LEFT:

Tjarnarskoli, Reyjavík
The Tjarnarskoli is a well-known elementary school building in Reykjavík, instantly recognizable by its yellow walls, red roof, and gothic-style tower. Education in Iceland is compulsory for children aged 6–16, the majority of the schools being state-run institutions.

OPPOSITE:

Old Harbour, Reykjavík
A rusting fishing vessel lies in the Old Harbour at Reykjavík. Despite a decline in fishing volumes since the 1970s, the industry still remains vitally important for Iceland, employing a total of 4.3 per cent of the country's workforce and generating 12 per cent of its gross domestic product.

LEFT:

Hallgrímskirkja, Reykjavík
The Hallgrímskirkja is a building of quite astonishing grace and a hard beauty, the vision of state architect Guðjón Samúelsson. Cast in an Expressionist style, yet fused with a deep connection to the Icelandic landscape, the building attracted much controversy during its construction, although today it is one of the city's leading landmarks.

RIGHT:

Hallgrímskirkja, Reykjavík
In this astonishing perspective on the Hallgrímskirkja, the lights of the *aurora borealis* play across the heavens above the cathedral's mighty tower. At 74.5m (244ft), the tower was deliberately designed to be taller than that of the Landakotskirkja (Landakot's Church).

LEFT:

Hallgrímskirkja, Reykjavík
The pipe organ inside the
Hallgrímskirkja was built by
the German organ builder
Johannes Klais of Bonn. It
is an astonishing work of
musical instrumentation –
15m (49ft) tall and weighing
25 tonnes (25 long tons; 28
short tons).

OPPOSITE:

**National Museum of
Iceland, Reykjavík**
An exquisite piece of early
Icelandic Christian art:
a detail from an embroidered
altar frontal from
Draflastaðir, north Iceland.
The official Christianization
of Iceland began in AD 1000,
although there had been
missionary outreach to the
island dating back to 980.
Prior to this time, the country
had been emphatically pagan.

Harpa, Reykjavík
The Harpa concert hall and conference centre is a modern fusion of glass and steel, designed by the firms Henning Larsen Architects and Batteríið Architects in co-operation with Danish-Icelandic artist Olafur Eliasson. Construction began in 2007. Following delays caused by the financial crash of 2008, it finally held its inaugural concert on 4 May 2011.

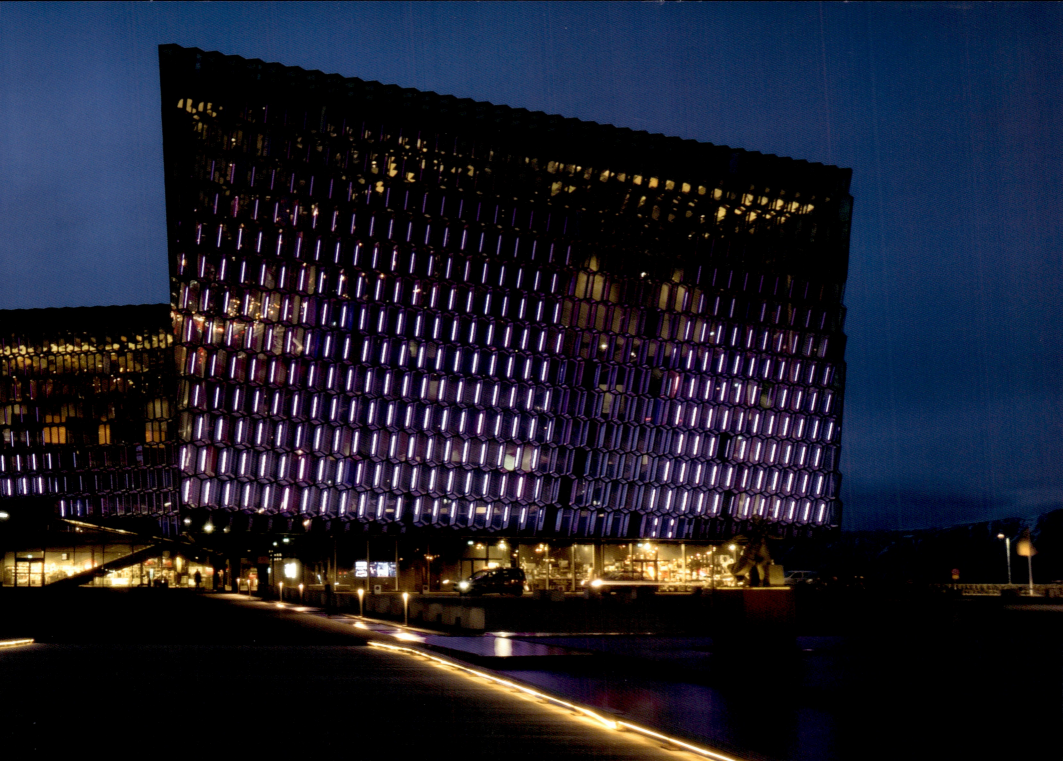

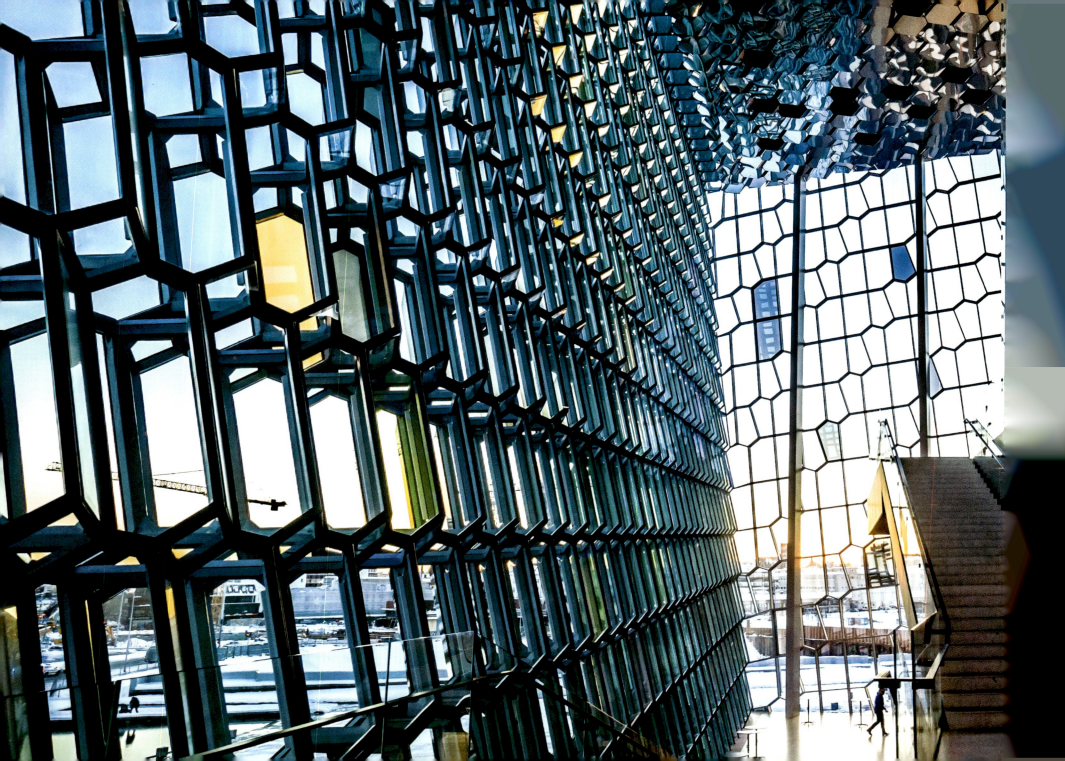

Harpa, Reykjavík
The Harpa concert hall plays constantly with the visual senses and with the viewer's understanding of perspective. It has what has been called a 'crystalline' layout, the patterns formed by the steelwork crossing geometric and more fluid structures.

LEFT:

Solfar the Sun Voyager, Reykjavík

Evoking the ancient days of Viking sail and oar, the sculpture *Solfar the Sun Voyager* by Jón Gunnar Árnason sits quietly by the sea in Reykjavík. The work, of stainless steel and granite slabs, was created in the 1980s. According to the artist, it suggests 'the promise of new, undiscovered territory'.

RIGHT:

Ásmundur Sveinsson Sculpture Museum, Reykjavík

Scattered artistic forms grace this room in the Ásmundur Sveinsson Sculpture Museum, on the outskirts of Reykjavík. Ásmundur Sveinsson (1893–1982), who both designed and worked in the museum building, was one of the great innovators in modern Icelandic sculpture.

LEFT:

Graffiti, Reykjavík
Often surprising to the overseas visitor, Reykjavík is the canvas for much high-quality graffiti and murals, created across the full range of size and scale. Here a monstrous robot crashes through a cityscape, pop art meeting disaster movie.

RIGHT:

Graffiti, Reykjavík
The graffiti of Reykjavík crosses all manner of styles and genres, from black-and-white fine art to the impressionistic swirls seen here. In a survey conducted for Bombing Science, an organization that explores international graffiti, Reykjavík was considered the ninth best city in the world for the art form.

Blue bike gate, Reykjavík

The Icelandic people are comfortable with combining artistic expression with straightforward practicality. Here an unwanted bike is turned into a road gate, creating in turn another great image for tourist photographs.

Graffiti, Reykjavík

Any plain wall surface in Reykjavík is likely to attract the graffiti artist's spray can or paint brush. Icelandic art wavered between abstract and figurative styles during the 20th century, and today both these styles, plus a myriad of other influences, can be seen on the fabric of the city.

OPPOSITE:

Graffiti, Reykjavík

Only for the hardiest of art enthusiasts, an abandoned chair invites the viewer to take a seat in the snow to study local graffiti in Reykjavík. Crime is extremely low in Iceland, so graffiti carries none of the gangland stigma attached to it in many other cities.

Graffiti, Reykjavík

The street of Grettisgata in central Reykjavík, little more than 100m (320ft) from the harbour front, is a desirable and attractive area. As with other neighbourhoods, its visual appeal is enhanced by the efforts of the local graffiti artists and painters.

Grotta, Seltjarnarnes

A singular image of isolation, Grotta is a tiny rocky islet at the western end of Reykjavík, in a nominal town called Seltjarnarnes. The patch of ground, frequently cut off by the tides around it, is home to a small lighthouse, which throws its welcome beams across the frigid waters of Faxafloi Bay. Because of its isolation, Grotta is a popular nesting site for sea birds.

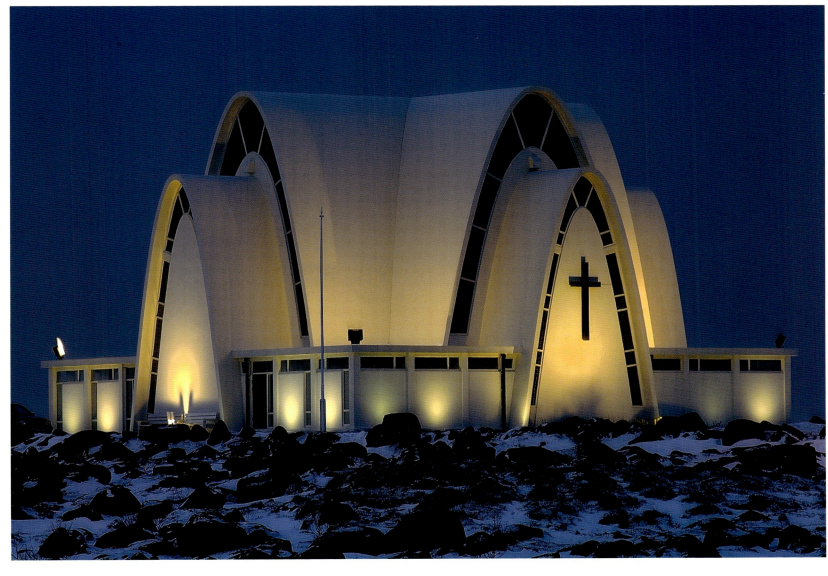

Rauðhólar, Southwest Iceland

The Rauðhólar ('red hills') appear as if spray painted against the grass and stone of nearby hills. They are a geological phenomenon known as pseudocraters, having the appearance of a volcanic structure but without an actual lava vent.

Kópavogskirkja, Kópavogur

The second-largest urban area in Iceland after Reykjavík, Kópavogur lies immediately to the south of the capital, and is home to c. 37,000 people. The strikingly modernist Kópavogskirkja was built between 1958 and 1962, its design dominated by arches and warm lighting effects.

Mosfellsbær Church, Mosfellsbær

Located just 12km (7 miles) east of Reykjavík, Mosfellsbær is set in a rugged landscape of hills, mountains and starkly beautiful valleys; the area is especially popular with outdoor sports enthusiasts. The historic Mosfellsbær Church is the epitome of spiritual refuge.

Hellisheiði Power Station, Hengill

Iceland fully capitalizes on geothermal energy, using it to provide more than 26 per cent of its electricity and to give 87 per cent of Icelandic homes hot water and central heating. The Hellisheiði Power Station (HGPS) in southwest Iceland delivers 303MW of electricity and 133MW of hot water to nearby Reykjavík.

Hellisheiði Power Station, Hengill

The Hellisheiði Power Station ranks as the third-largest geothermal power station in the world, an engineering triumph and a model of sustainable energy that began electricity production in 2006, and opened its hot-water plant in 2010. The energy comes from 30 wells bored 2000–3000m (6561–9842ft) down into the Icelandic rock.

Keflavík International Airport, Keflavík

Keflavík International Airport had its origins back in World War II, when a runway and base facilities were constructed by the US military. To this day, parts of the airport are still given to military use, but the civilian services began to run in the 1980s. One of the advantages of Keflavík is its two 3000m (9840ft) runways, long enough to land any aircraft, even the Space Shuttle.

Blue Lagoon, Reykjanes Peninsula

The Blue Lagoon is one of Iceland's most compelling physical attractions. A vast spa, heated by geothermal energy, its waters are at an average of 39°C (102°F), including during the freezing winter months; hence it is a year-round destination for locals and tourists.

In addition to their heat, the Blue Lagoon's waters are also rich in skin-friendly minerals, which give the lake its vibrant blue colour. Many people travel to bathe in the lake for medicinal purposes. Because of natural circulation, the water in the lake is renewed every 48 hours.

Blue Lagoon, Reykjanes Peninsula

A couple share a moment of ultimate relaxation under the bridge in the Blue Lagoon. A common misconception is that the lake is natural; in fact, the heated water comes from the nearby Svartsengi geothermal power plant.

Brimketill, Reykjanes Peninsula

Its appearance changing dramatically throughout the year, from placid summer pond to boiling winter cauldron, the Brimketill is a large natural pool carved out of the Icelandic lava rock by the repetitive blows of the sea. Folklore speaks of the giantess Oddný taking baths in the pool.

Bridge Between Continents, Reykjanes Peninsula
Although the grand 'Bridge Between Continents' label clashes somewhat with its functional appearance, this 15m (49ft) footbridge actually crosses the tectonic plate boundary between Eurasia and North America. The Reykjanes Peninsula is set directly on the Mid-Atlantic Ridge.

Grindavík, Reykjanes Peninsula

The village of Grindavík nestles in the far southwest of Iceland. It is a place of outstanding natural beauty, with a breathtaking coastline. The coast is also a dangerous one for shipping. Here is the wreck of *Hrafn Sveinbjarnarson III GK-11*, which became stranded and lost in February 1988 (all the crew were rescued).

RIGHT:

Hópsnes Lighthouse, near Grindavík, Reykjanes Peninsula

Hópsnes Lighthouse sits on a spit of land 2km (1.2 miles) long and 1km (0.6 miles) wide. It was built in 1928, primarily to give guidance to the numerous fishing boats plying the coast during the night-time hours or when thick fog or snowy white-outs descended.

Mt Keilir, Reykjanes Peninsula
Almost giving the appearance of a shark's fin cuting through
a marbled ocean, Mt Keilir is a volcanic mountain southwest
of Hafnarfjörður, and a key landmark on the Reykjanes
Peninsula. It is not a tall mountain – just 250m (820ft) in
elevation – but it is still a hearty two- or three-hour climb
to its summit.

Festarfjall, Reykjanes Peninsula
The Festarfjall is an eroded subglacial volcano in the
Reykjanes Peninsula. Much of the landscape of Iceland is the
legacy, or the continuing presence, of volcanic activity. Legend
has it that a dyke running through the lava sequence is actually
the necklace of a she-troll.

OPPOSITE:

Reykjanes Peninsula

The economic life of the Reykjanes Peninsula was for a long time centred upon fishing, which still occupies many of the inhabitants today. These wooden scaffolds are for fish drying and smoking, the dried fish providing a durable source of protein that lasts throughout the winter months.

RIGHT:

Seltún Geothermal Area, Reykjanes Peninsula

An extraordinary example of Iceland's living landscape, the Seltún is about 40km (25 miles) from Reykjavík. The geothermal energy beneath the rock produces surface effects that include steaming rivers and bubbling mud pools, the rocks often around coloured brightly by natural chemical deposits.

The Old Lighthouse, Garður
The town of Garður is on the northern tip of the Reykjanes
Peninsula. Its location next to some of the Peninsula's best
fishing grounds meant that Garður was in times past a
heavily populated village. Today Garður is best known for the
plentiful and diverse local wildlife, and its spectacular views
out over the sea.

Stafnes Lighthouse, Reykjanes Peninsula
Iceland's coastline is dotted with lighthouses, bastions of light
in a hard coastal landscape. Their locations mean that they
often see the fullness of Iceland's atmospheric effects, such as
this truly magical ripple of the Northern Lights above Stafnes
Lighthouse in the Reykjanes Peninsula.

Southern Region

The Southern Region of Iceland is a place both wild and welcoming in equal measures. It features some of the island's most popular natural landmarks, partly courtesy of its proximity to Reykjavík (which acts as the base for many tourists), but principally because of the region's scale, grandeur and timeless beauty.

Southern Iceland is bordered by the North Atlantic Ocean, which through eons of relentless pounding and erosion has crafted a coastal landscape of drama and beauty, defined by towering basalt pillars, rocky arches, rock pools and teeming bird life. Iceland's volanic foundations also mean that the sand and shingle of many beaches are a deep, rich black, contrasting like long rivers of ink against the white crashing surf or the winter ice. Beyond the coastline, heading into the interior and up towards the Highlands, we meet a landscape still very much in the process of forming. Glaciers, mountains, geysers, valleys, thundering waterfalls – there is something to rejuvenate and inspire every tired modern eye. For those wishing to explore southern Iceland, the 'Golden Circle' is often the most accessible option: a 300-km (186-mile) route around the three most popular natural attractions in Iceland: the Geysir Geothermal Area, Gullfoss Waterfall and Thingvellir National Park. It is a journey around a largely untouched world, experiencing nature at its most elemental.

OPPOSITE:
Strokkur, Haukadalur
The Strokkur geyser is located in the Haukadalur geothermal region of southern Iceland. For c. 800 years, every 5–10 minutes, the geyser has been throwing jets of heated water up into the air, rising up to 30m (98ft).

Álftavatn Lake, Southern Iceland

Álftavatn Lake (Swan Lake) is a place of spectral beauty in the Icelandic Highlands, accessible only by four-wheel-drive vehicle along the tough Syðri Fjallabak track, open from July to late September, or along the Laugavegur hiking trail. According to legend, an Icelandic man drowned in the lake in the 18th century, but his spirit appeared to his wife in a dream and told her where they could find his body.

Dyrhólaey Lighthouse, Southern Iceland

Dyrhólaey Lighthouse, here seen leaning against the icy
Atlantic winds, sits more than 100m (328ft) above the sea.
Although fully operational as a lighthouse, the building has
also been transformed into a small boutique hotel, sleeping up
to five people. The town of Vík – Iceland's southernmost town
– is about 15 minutes' drive from Dyrhólaey.

Dyrhólaey, Southern Iceland

Dyrhólaey presents one of the most dramatic coastal
images Iceland has to offer. Located 174km (108 miles) from
Reykjavík, Dyrhólaey's name – meaning 'the hill island with
the hole' – comes from the magisterial arch of black lava rock
that straddles the sea. The area teems with wildlife and the
rocky cliffs are major nesting grounds for puffins.

Brúarfoss Waterfall, Southern Iceland

Brúarfoss (Bridge Falls) waterfall is a step down in the flow of the glacial River Brúará. Although the drop of the waterfall is minor – about 3m (9ft) – the intensely pure, blue water creates a magical effect for the viewer.

OPPOSITE:

Fjaðrárgljúfur, Southeast Iceland

Another of Iceland's many geographical hidden gems, the Fjaðrárgljúfur is an untouched and picturesque canyon running for about 2km (1.2 miles) at a depth of around 100m (328ft). It is a winding and sinuous canyon, laced through at the bottom with the River Fjaðrá.

LEFT:

Eyjafjallajökull, Southwest Iceland

Viewed here from the plain below, Eyjafjallajökull (Island Mountain Glacier) is essentially a volcano topped by a dramatic ice cap, the volcano reaching an elevation of 1651m (5417ft) at its summit. The ice cap itself spreads out over an area of 100 sq km (39 sq miles), while the crater is 3–4km (1.9–2.5 miles) in diameter.

ABOVE:

Eyjafjallajökull, Southwest Iceland

The Eyjafjallajökull volcano is still very much active, the deep rumblings and numerous minor earthquakes in the region testifying to its restlessness. On 20 March 2010, the volcano erupted with an explosive roar, and the ash subsequently pumped into the atmosphere affected aircraft flights across Europe for months.

LEFT:

**Eyrarbakki,
Southwest Iceland**
Eyrarbakki is a coastal town
of c. 600 souls, and was
formerly a major trading
hub between Iceland and
Denmark. The nearby
beaches are formed of a black
volcanic sand, which at low
tide creates almost spine-like
patterns as the water retreats.

OPPOSITE:

**Gullfoss Waterfall,
Southwest Iceland**
The Gullfoss Waterfall is
a spectacular, thundering
natural display, the
meltwaters of Iceland's
second biggest glacier, the
Langjökull, falling a
distance of 32m (105ft)
into the base of the valley.
In deep winter even these
fast-flowing waters freeze
over, creating immense
structures of hanging ice.

**Hraungerðiskirkja,
Hraungerði**

The Hraungerðiskirkja is a
classically picturesque church
in southern Iceland. The
Hraungerði site has evidence
of church-building going back
to the 13th century, although
the Hraungerðiskirkja itself
was consecrated in 1902.

RIGHT:

**Hraungerðiskirkja,
Hraungerði**

The interior of the
Hraungerðiskirkja shuns all
ecclesiastical austerity, instead
embracing warm colours
and a ceiling vault that lifts
the eyes heavenwards. The
architect was Eiríkur Gíslason
from Bitru.

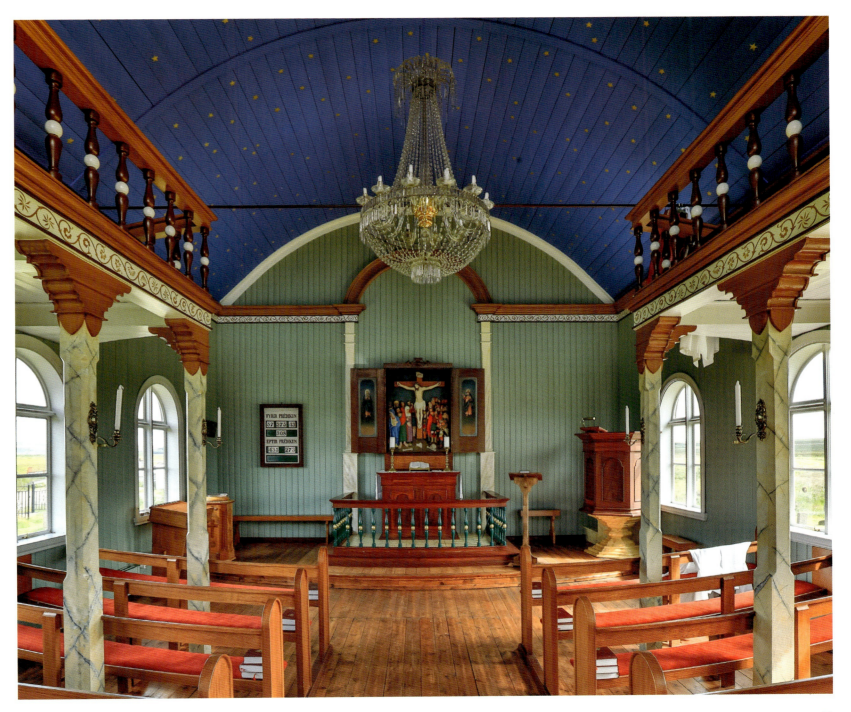

Hvolsvöllur, Southwest Iceland

A small Lutheran church near the town of Hvolsvöllur stands as a beacon of light in the winter snowscape. Hvolsvöllur itself has a population of c. 900 inhabitants, and is about 100km (62 miles) southeast of Reykjavík. The name of the town translates as 'Hill Field', and the region is the setting for the 13th-century Icelandic saga known as *Njál's Saga*.

Remundargil Canyon, South Iceland
Sitting on the Golden Circle route in southern Iceland, and
looking verdant without its winter casing of ice and snow,
the Remundargil Canyon presents a spectacular landscape
of mountains, valleys and waterfalls. The green covering is
actually created by a thick layer of moss.

ABOVE:

Kerið, Grímsnes, South Iceland
Kerið is a volanic crater lake, located in Iceland's Western
Volcanic Zone. The lake at the bottom of the impressive
caldera is not deep – maximum depth is about 14m (46ft)
– but the caldera itself is 55m (180ft) deep and 270m
(890ft) in circumference.

Kerlingarfjöll, Highlands

Kerlingarfjöll, or the Ogress' Mountains, is set in the centre of the Icelandic Highlands. The mountains cluster together, multiple summits and ridges vying for attention. Trails are laid across the peaks and through the valleys, most of them winding across the landscape at altitudes of more than 1000m (3280ft).

Kirkjusandur, near Dyrhólaey

Kirkjusandur beach appears here like a vast, thick oil slick, the black volcanic sand oozing out from the coastline behind. Although the beach is popular with tourists, it can also be dangerous, subject to sudden massive waves, and fatalities are not uncommon.

Landmannalaugar, Southern Highlands

Landmannalaugar, an area of mountains and deeply cut
fissures and valleys, presents an extraordinary vision of
geological time and power. The colours in the rocks are due
to moss and to the rhyolite stone, which can present itself in a
variety of red, pink, green, blue and golden-yellow hues.

Landmannalaugar, Southern Highlands

This ice cave, thinning under the spring sunshine, creates the
appearance of icy cathedral vaults. Landmannalaugar sits at the
northern end of the Laugavegur, one of Iceland's most popular
hiking trails, and sightseers frequent the landscape during the
warmer months.

Langjökull Glacier, Western Highlands

Langjökull glacier is a mighty feature of the Icelandic Highlands, the second-largest glacier on the island, measuring 935 sq km (361 sq miles). Its dimensions, considering that it is a vast, moving plain of ice, never fail to impress: 50km (31 miles) long and up to 20km (12 miles) wide. The ice itself is up to 580m (1903ft) deep, providing ample material for carving out ice tunnels, another popular part of the tourist trail.

Raufarhólshellir, Southwest Iceland
Here appearing more like a fantasy film set than a naturally occurring phenomenon, the Raufarhólshellir is a lava tunnel that takes the visitor into the heart of an Icelandic volcano. The crystalline columns on the floor are pillars of ice, which form in the tunnels every winter.

Reynisdrangar Sea Cliffs, Southern Iceland
The Reynisdrangar cliffs are towering columns of basalt rock rising out of the shoreline sea near the village of Vík in Myrdal. Here they are photographed with a long exposure, revealing the Milky Way above in the exceptionally clear Icelandic skies.

ABOVE:

Reynisfjara Beach, Southern Iceland
Reynisfjara Beach is a place of poetic beauty, recognized by
the fact that in 1991 *National Geographic* magazine voted
it in the Top 10 of the planet's most beautiful non-tropical
beaches. It has to be respected, however – its waves are fast
and treacherous.

OPPOSITE:

Reynisfjara Beach, Southern Iceland
With its distinctive black beaches, created by millions of years
of time grinding down volanic rocks, Reynisfjara Beach is a
primordial landscape. Time and the elements have also created
the famous stacks of basalt rock, here appearing like hundreds
of architectural pillars.

ABOVE:

Sólheimasandur, Southern Iceland
The beach at Sólheimasandur is famous for the wreck of a US
Navy DC-3 aircraft, which crash-landed on the coast in 1973.
Reports of the cause of the crash are scant, but it appears that
the accident was caused by running out of fuel. Fortunately, all
of the crew survived the incident.

RIGHT:

Seljalandsfoss Waterfall, Southern Iceland
In this scene of natural perfection, the Seljalandsfoss Waterfall
roars off the cliffs, falling 60m (197ft) to the floor below
while the Northern Lights trace magical green patterns in the
skies above. A path loops fully around the waterfall, enabling
visitors to walk behind the cascade.

LEFT:

Seljavallalaug, near Ásólfsskáli
A hardy soul takes a dip in the outdoor pool of Seljavallalaug, located in the mountains some 10km (6 miles) east of Ásólfsskáli. The pool was constructed back in 1923 as a facility to teach Icelandic children how to swim, and it has changed little since.

OPPOSITE:

Skálholt, Southwest Iceland
Throughout much of Iceland's history, Skálholt was a major religious, cultural and political centre. Although its importance declined, a large cathedral still towers over the site, and these two sculptures in the cathedral grounds evoke the figures and personalities of the past.

Western Region

The Western Region of Iceland perfectly represents the continuity and contrasts of Iceland, although to outsiders it is generally not as well known as the more southerly regions around Reykjavík. Much of its geographical area is in the Snæfellsnes Peninsula, home to one of Iceland's three national parks. Here nature explores its possibilities in unbounded fashion, in mountains, rivers, gorges, lava fields and bold coastlines. Landmarks include the Hraunfossar waterfalls, the Djúpalónssandur ('Black Lava Pearl Beach') and the Snæfellsjökull glacier, towering to such height that on clear days it can even be seen from Reykjavík, nearly 200km (124 miles) to the south.

But even apparently timeless landmarks speak of change, to which Iceland is not immune. In August 2012, for example, locals noted with concern that the peak of the glacier had no snow or ice, a historical first; global warming reaches even this far north. Yet the beautiful towns and villages of the region still throb to the engines of fishing vessels, which carve out their living from the icy seas. Today, cruise liners also grace the ports, with all their ambiguous blessings. Yet even as tourist numbers grow, the remoteness of this spectacular region means that it remains a place where visitors and locals alike can find peace and solitude, and endless beauty whatever the season or the mood.

OPPOSITE:
Akranes, West Iceland
Lying just 49km (30 miles) north of the centre of Reykjavík, Akranes is a town of c. 7000 people, set between the fjords of Hvalfjörður and Borgarfjörður. The town grew on the back of the fishing industry, which remains the cornerstone of the local economy. Rusting fishing boats of yesteryear still lie around the harbour and foreshore.

ALL:
Bjarnarhöfn, Snæfellsnes Peninsula

The Bjarnarhöfn Shark Museum is a working museum dedicated to explaining the ecology, harvesting and production of *hákarl* (fermented shark meat), a traditional Icelandic delicacy, albeit not one to everyone's taste. The fermentation process, performed in the sheds seen here, is critical, as the flesh of the Greenland shark is actually poisonous if not treated.

LEFT:

Dried fish, Western Iceland

Dried fish is something of a rarity in western Europe, but in Iceland it has been a traditional part of the diet for centuries. Drying racks such as this one expose the fish to the fresh, salty air, steadily removing the water content. Once dried, the fish can be stored for many months without refrigeration.

TOP RIGHT:

Angler fish, Western Iceland

Iceland has numerous species of edible fish in its water, offering something for every different palate. Here we see an angler fish, which in its largest varieties can reach 0.6m (2ft) in length and weigh up to 40kg (88lb)

BOTTOM RIGHT:

Drying rack, Western Iceland

A traditional drying rack by the side of the ocean features a variety of sea creatures. When a fish is dried out, it loses about 80 per cent of its weight, thus dried fish is easy both to transport and to store. When it comes time for the fish to be eaten, soaking and beating will make the flesh soft again for consumption.

LEFT:
Búðakirkja, Snæfellsnes Peninsula

Here presenting a rather unnvering, almost supernatural, sight, the 'Black Church' is located in the Búðahraun lava field. The first church at this location was built in 1703, but the present church dates from just 1987, erected following the petitions of one parishioner.

RIGHT:
Djúpalónssandur, Snæfellsnes Peninsula

The Djúpalónssandur ('Black Lava Pearl Beach') is a bay on the Snæfellsnes Peninsula, its arcing contours described in black volcanic rock. One interesting discovery on the beach was four ancient lifting stones, used to test the strength of fishermen. They weigh from 23kg (50lb) to 155kg (342lb).

ALL:

Hraunfossar Waterfalls, Borgarfjordur

The Hraunfossar (Lava Falls) are a refreshing natural phenomenon located on the edge of the the Hallmundarhraun lava field. Pure spring water pushes its way through the lava rock in a series of springs; when it emerges – as if from nowhere – it forms multiple cascades, running a distance of 90m (300ft) across the moss-covered stones into the River Hvítá. The rushing noise of the water, exceptional purity of the water, and the colour of the rocks and river bed create a calming aesthetic effect.

Snæfellsnes Peninsula, Western Iceland
An aerial photograph shows the grandeur of the Snæfellsnes Peninsula, with muscular mountains hunched up around the coastline. The covering of snow here obscures the fact that the Peninsula has some golden sandy beaches, in contrast to the black lava sand forming many other Icelandic beaches.

OPPOSITE:

Snæfellsnes Peninsula, Western Iceland

The jagged coastline of the Snæfellsnes Peninsula has required some bold thinking in terms of road planning, evident in this dramatic causeway. The Snæfellsnes Peninsula overall is 90km (56 miles) long, and most of the populated areas straddle the northern coastline and the western tip.

ABOVE:

Snæfellsnes Peninsula, Western Iceland

An abandoned farm sits in a chilly hilltop location in the Snæfellsnes Peninsula, the arctic winds blowing freely through its empty shell. At the westernmost part of the Peninsula is the Snæfellsjökull National Park, a concentrated space of wildlife and natural beauty.

Grundarfjörður, Snæfellsnes Peninsula
Grundarfjörður offers welcoming warmth and light during the winter months in Western Iceland. With a population of c. 1000, the town sits in the centre of the Snæfellsnes Peninsula's northern coastline. In addition to visitors who drive in by car, Grundarfjörður is also a popular destination with cruise lines.

**Stykkishólmur,
Snæfellsnes Peninsula**

Stykkishólmur is located by
Breiðafjörður Bay on the
northern tip of Snæfellsnes
Peninsula; it is the Peninsula's
capital. As much as its
stunning backdrop catches
the eye, its colourful and
award-winning housing
also appeals to the senses.
The town has grown over
recent years, fuelled by a
combination of tourism,
investment and civic pride.

LEFT:

**Ólafsvík Church,
Snæfellsnes Peninsula**
The Ólafsvíkurkirkja
(Ólafsvík Church) is
undeniably modern in
appearance, testimony to
the architectural revolution
sweeping church design
during the 1960s (it was
consecrated in 1967). Yet
for all its modernity, it still
manages to feel neither dated
nor out of place with its
natural surroundings.

RIGHT:

**Stykkishólmur,
Snæfellsnes Peninsula**
The Stykkishólmskirkja
is immediately arresting,
looming over the coast of
the Snæfellsnes Peninsula.
Consecrated in 1990, it was
designed by architect Jón
Haraldsson. The salient
feature is the bold bell tower,
inspired by whale vertebrae.

**Ólafsvík,
Snæfellsnes Peninsula**
With its large harbour, Ólafsvík's life has been defined by the rhythms of the sea and the fishing industry. It is located in the northwest of the Snæfellsnes Peninsula, 195km (121 miles) from Reykjavík. While the sea borders the town to the north, inland it is close to the Snæfellsjökull glacier, an ice-capped volcano rising 1446m (4744ft) over Western Iceland.

Westfjords

Studying the map of Iceland draws the eye inexorably up to the north and west, to the projecting territory of the Westfjords. In this expansive, remote peninsula, the land and the sea are equal partners, the latter etching the former with bays and fjords – including some of the biggest in Iceland – while the coastline resists the drumbeat of the ocean waves with towering cliffs and coastal mountains.

Although cruise liners occasionally dip into its waterways, the Westfjords is known for its imperious isolation. The region has a total area of 22,271 sq km (8599 sq miles), but its population is just c. 7300, scattered between a small number of larger towns and a far larger number of minor settlements, some of these populated by just a single family or handful of farmers and fishermen. Because of the Westfjords' remoteness, however, the territory is a veritable playground for wildlife, especially seabirds – Látrabjarg cliffs alone are home to literally millions of puffins and other birds – but also arctic foxes and hares.

In times past, the Westfjords had a major whaling industry, using the fjords as bases from which to hunt the great creatures out in the open sea. Whaling has not disappeared entirely from Iceland, although it has been drastically reduced, but whale watching for tourists has become a service industry in its own right.

OPPOSITE:
Rauðasandur, Látrabjarg Peninsula
Home primarily to wildlife, especially the seabirds and seals
that teem onshore and offshore, the Rauðasandur (Red Sand)
beach occupies an idyllic and often deserted 10km (6 miles)
of the coastline in the southwest of the Westfjords.

Drangaskörð, Westfjords
The aptly named Drangaskörð (Dragon's Tail) is a looming and jagged promontory of rock located in the northwest of the Westfjords, the 'tail' of the nearby Skarðafjall Mountain. The individual rocks are given the names of ghosts in Icelandic legend.

OPPOSITE:

Hólmavík, Strandir Region, Westfjords

Icelandic nature is hard on manmade structures, as indicated by these cabins rusting rapidly on the salty shoreline at Hólmavík, in the north of the Westfjords. Hólmavík is an isolated town with a population of c. 500. Buses between the town and Reykjavík run only two–four times each week, the timetables altering according to the seasons.

ABOVE, TOP RIGHT AND BOTTOM RIGHT:

Hólmavík, Strandir Region, Westfjords

Hólmavík is a hub for fishing in the Westfjords; sheep farming is another core element of the town's economy. The town also has something of a dark and mystical past – some 20 locals were burnt at the stake here during the Icelandic witch hunts of the 17th century – reflected in the popular Museum of Sorcery & Witchcraft.

Hornstrandir Nature Reserve, Westfjords
The Hornstrandir Nature Research is the northernmost projection of the Westfjords. Its remoteness is absolute, with very few inhabitants or settlements; thus it offers near-unrivalled opportunities to see nature in the raw, without human intrusions. Offshore tours enable visitors to observe its vertiginous cliffs with little effort.

Lighthouse, Westfjords
An old lighthouse testifies to the effects of time and weather as it stands on a bleak coastline in the Westfjords. Shipwrecks dot the coastline of the Westfjords, driven onto the rocks by waves, wind, currents and navigational errors.

ABOVE:
Kleifabúi Cairn, Kleifaheiði Pass
The Kleifabúi cairn was built from local stones by road workers constructing a road across the Kleifaheiði Pass in the Westfjords.

RIGHT:
Ísafjörður, northern Westfjords
With a population of c. 2600, and a setting of spectacular visual grandeur, Ísafjörður is the largest habitation in the Wesfjords, and a popular base for exploring the surrounding landscapes.

Skotufjordur, Westfjords

A pristine expanse of water, the Skotufjordur (Sting Ray Bay) stretches 16km (10 miles) through the northern Westfjords. The environment is superb for fostering wildlife, particularly birds such as white tailed eagle, gyrfalcon, eider duck and numerous types of waders and plovers.

Bolafjall Mountain, Bolungarvík

The radar station atop Bolafjall Mountain was originally one of four early-warning radar sites operated by the US military on Iceland, although now it is in the hands of the Icelandic Coast Guard. The mountain itself has an elevation of 638m (2093ft), overlooking Bolungarvík village.

Látrabjarg, Westfjords

The cliffs of Látrabjarg, 14km (9 miles) long and up to 441m (1447ft) high, confront the first-time visitor with a natural spectacle with few rivals. Literally millions of sea birds, mostly puffins, cling to the cliffs, the numbers defying comprehension. The cliffs are a perfect habitat for the birds, the vertiginous walls protecting the birds against most land predators.

Flatey Island, Breiðafjörður Bay

Flatey Island – aptly meaning 'Flat Island' – is one of about 40 islands dotted around the northern Westfjords. The isolation of the island means that it has (at the time of writing) just two farmers living there, with one dog. Nevertheless, the island has a small seasonal hotel for visitors.

Súðavík, Westfjords
Súðavík's stirring location has, on occasions in the past, been its curse. In 1995, a large part of the village was wiped out in an avalanche running off the surrounding mountains. Nevertheless, the village still thrives today, with a new part (safe from avalanches) built to house visitors in the winter, the old part for summer visitors, and several well-established service businesses.

OPPOSITE:

Ísafjarðardjúp, Westfjords
A commercial fishing trawler makes way under a gathering storm in the Ísafjarðardjúp (Icefjord's Deep). The Ísafjarðardjúp is such a vast body of water – it almost splits the Westfjords in two – that it is actually divided into eight sub fjords.

OPPOSITE:

Samúel Jónsson Art Museum, Selárdalur

Samúel Jónsson (1884–1969) was an Icelandic artist of unfettered vision. Up until his retirement at the age of 65, Jónsson's life was a hard one, largely spent in farming, but retirement (and the accompanying pension) gave him the time and funds to explore his unique brand of art. The restored building seen here is the church built by Jónsson.

TOP LEFT:

Samúel Jónsson Art Museum, Selárdalur

Jónsson's abstract view on the world was expressed particularly through sculpture, which today mostly sits in the garden behind the museum building. Both art and building were rotting away following Jónsson's death, but the work of local restoration groups has brought the site and its artworks back to their full glory and colour.

BOTTOM LEFT AND TOP RIGHT:

Samúel Jónsson Art Museum, Selárdalur

The building seen bottom left is Jónsson's own home, prior to its restoration. Following the restoration efforts, the house more fully reflects Jónsson's artistry and abstract view of the world (top left, top right). Jónsson did not achieve high artistic status either in life or after his death, but he is held up as a quirky exponent of Icelandic folk art.

OPPOSITE:

Mjóifjörður, Westfjords

A shipwreck lies in the Mjóifjörður (Narrow Fjord), a thin 18-km (11-mile) long stretch of water between the Norðfjörður and Seyðisfjörður. The ship was once a former Norwegian whaling trawler; the Norwegians had a major whaling base located in the Mjóifjörður in the early 20th century.

RIGHT:

Hvalfjörður, Westfjords

The Hvalfjörður (Whale Fjord) cuts deep into the Westfjords, its entrance just 50km (31 miles) to the north of Reykjavík. As suggested by its name, the fjord used to be a centre for whaling activities. During World War II, both the British and the US navies used the Hvalfjörður as a deep-water base, supporting its trans-Atlantic convoy activities; the rusting pier is a legacy of that past.

Flatey Island, Breiðafjörður Bay

Flatey Island has numerous creaking shipwrecks dotted along the shoreline and coastal waters, of ages ranging from modern vessels to old wooden sail boats. One wreck in Flatey Harbour – the *Melkmeid* (Milkmaid) – sank there in 1659 as it wrestled against a severe Icelandic storm. Thankfully, all but one of the crew survived the sinking.

Skápadalur Valley, Patreksfjörður

The *Garðar BA 64* was a former whaling ship, built and launched in Norway 1912 as the *Globe IV* but subsequently sold to several fleets. It entered Icelandic service just after World War II, taking its final name in 1963 and becoming a fishing trawler as restrictions on whaling took hold. It was rammed ashore in 1981 and left to rust away.

LEFT:

**Vigur Island,
Ísafjörður Bay**

Only a single family live tenaciously on the island of Vigur, amid large colonies of puffins, eider ducks, arctic terns, black guillemots, razorbills and other seabirds. The family members actually harvest down from the birds' nests to make products such as duvets and pillows. The mill on Vigur is the only preserved wind-powered grain mill in Iceland, the first such mill built on the site in 1860.

OPPOSITE:

Dynjandi, Westfjords

The Dynjandi waterfall, between Dynjandisvogur Bay and Arnarfjörður fjord, delivers a breathtaking spectacle. Spilling over the cliffs, the waterfall cascades a distance of 100m (328ft) in a broad swathe 60m (196ft) wide at the bottom, likened to a huge bridal veil. The translation of its name is apt – 'Thunderous'.

Northern Region

The Northern Region of Iceland is a territory in which nature is unleashed in its most elemental forms, with landscapes that appear of a time before humans even walked upon the Earth. Vast lava fields and volcanic landscapes; waterfalls of unimaginable power; coastlines hewn by time and tide from basalt rock; seas and fjords in which whales breach and sing. It is a world of natural extremes, and a testimony to the fact that Iceland straddles one of the most active volcanic regions of the world. Such sights are an irresistible draw for the adventurous, scientific and the artistic.

Yet Northern Iceland is not just about its natural elements, but also about the humans who live there. The region has a major city in the form of Akureyri, the second largest urban area after Reykjavík, plus numerous smaller towns and villages, all with their own distinct identities and pastimes. Traditional crafts abound on large and small scales, and Iceland's architects have created buildings here that both complement and defy Iceland's unforgiving climate and landscape. Northern Iceland is a place where hardy people have hewn not just a living from land and sea, but also cultures of their own.

OPPOSITE:
Goðafoss Waterfall, River Skjálfandafljót
The Goðafoss waterfall ranks among the most spectacular of the Icelandic cascades. Its drop is just 12m (39ft), but it is 30m (98ft) wide, creating a visual impact that does full justice to its translated name – 'Waterfall of the Gods'.

**Herðubreið,
Northeast Iceland**
For some, Herðubreið is the
defining mountain of Iceland.
Geologically, it is a tuya, a
flat-topped but steep-sided
volcano, formed when a
great column of lava erupts
up through a glacier or ice
sheet, and cools rapidly. In
translation it is called 'Broad
Shouldered', and it rises
imperiously to an elevation
of 1677m (5501ft) above the
surrounding lava field.

BELOW:

Hofsós Swimming Pool, Hofsós

Surely few swimming pools in the world have a view as unique and inspiring as that at Hofsós. It was designed by the same architect responsible for Iceland's famous Blue Lagoon; he placed the small pool right up to the sea's edge, almost giving the impression of a vast infinity pool.

OPPOSITE:

Kálfshamarsvík, Skagi Peninsula

Representing the effects of two million years of geological time, the basalt cliffs at Kálfshamarsvík Cove are a sight of wonder. There was a nearby fishing village of Kálfshamarsvík, thriving during the early 1900s, but today it is deserted, leaving a few abandoned houses.

LEFT:

Hveravellir, Central Highlands

The Hveravellir (Hot Spring Fields) nature reserve is a bubbling and pictureque geothermal area in the Icelandic Highlands, nestling 650m (2132ft) above sea level. Geysers and naturally occurring hot pools, some at an ideal temperature for bathing, proliferate in a rocky wilderness with inspiring views.

ABOVE:

Hvítserkur, Vatnsnes Peninsula

Legend has it that the Hvítserkur – actually part of a sea-eroded volcano of long ago – is the body of a giant troll, locked into rocky form when he was caught in the petrifying sunlight, while mischievously trying to rip down the bells of a nearby convent.

LEFT:

Akureyrarkirkja, Akureyri
Iceland is a land of churches, offering spiritual and physical refuge in a landscape that can be tough on people and minds. The Lutheran Akureyrarkirkja is one of the most impressive such buildings on the northern coastline, designed by Guðjón Samúelsson and consecrated in 1940.

OPPOSITE TOP:

Blönduós Kirkja, Blönduós
The Blönduós Kirkja almost seems to form itself out of the lava that still moulds the contours of the island. The designer, Dr. Maggi Jónsson, took his inspiration from the shape of a volcano.

OPPOSITE BOTTOM LEFT:

Akureyrarkirkja, Akureyri
An interior view of the Akureyrarkirkja. Features of the church include a pipe organ with 3200 pipes and a model ship suspended from the ceiling – the latter making an old pagan reference to blessing those at sea.

OPPOSITE BOTTOM RIGHT:

Saudaneskirkja Church, Langanes Peninsula
The Saudaneskirkja Church reflects the humble, unpretentious style of many small Icelandic churches, the surrounding landscape often delivering the numinous grandeur.

LEFT:

**Skagafjörður,
Northern Iceland**
Horse trekking is a
popular pursuit around the
spectacular Skagafjörður, and
the area is further known for
its equine breeding activities.
The region also offers, for
those who lean towards more
extreme sports, some of
the best white-water rafting
experiences on the island.

OPPOSITE:

**Skagafjörður,
Northern Iceland**
The statue of Jón Ósmann,
a famous local ferryman,
overlooks the Skagafjörður,
the figure acting as a sentinel
for those traversing the river.
Ósmann manned a ferry
across the waters for many
years, until a bridge over
Vesturós was built in 1926.

ABOVE:

Dimmuborgir, Lake Mývatn area

Lava has crafted every manner of shape and contour in the Icelandic wilderness. The Dimmuborgir, or the Black Fortress, was formed during an eruption 2300 years ago, when rivers of lava came into contact with a lake, causing the molten rock to harden quickly into what locals see as a castle-like structure.

RIGHT:

Aldeyjarfoss, Highlands

The Aldeyjarfoss is a magnificent waterfall in the northern Highlands. The geological structures of the canyon walls, however, vie for attention with the waterfall, their characteristic honeycombs and columns of basalt giving the rockfaces an almost industrial appearance in places.

Bjarnarflag, Námaskarð

The Bjarnarflag geothermal power station opened in 1969, making it the oldest such powerplant in Iceland. It is in the Námaskarð hot spring area, a volatile region known for its seismic activity – the power station has been closed on several occasions because of earthquakes.

RIGHT:

Hvammstangi, Vatnsnes Peninsula

Hvammstangi has a thousand years of history behind it as a settlement, although its rise as a modern trading centre dates back to the 19th century. Today it has restaurants, shops and many other facilities for locals and tourists alike, with superb opportunities for seal watching.

Sheep Pen, Northern Iceland
Sheep farming is an important industry to Iceland, bearing in mind that the island has 800,000 sheep compared to 339,000 people. Pens like these are used for the *réttir* (corral) that occurs around September, when the sheep are gathered in from the surrounding countryside and collected in a specific location.

LEFT:
Sheep, Northern Iceland
Icelandic sheep breeds are especially hardy creatures, able to survive the harshest of outdoor climates. The sheep are mostly bred for their lamb meat, but also their wool – Icelanders are passionate about the craft of knitting.

OPPOSITE:

Sheep gathering, Northern Iceland

The autumnal gathering of the sheep, or *smölun* (the *réttir* refers to the collection of the sheep in one place), is not just a practical task but also a social event, bringing together many farmers and islanders. During the last day of the *réttir*, a celebratory atmosphere develops, with much singing and drinking.

RIGHT, ALL:

KIDKA Wool Factory, Hvammstangi

The KIDKA wool factory is one of the biggest knitting factories in Iceland, producing all types of woollen gifts and garments, including hats, scarves, jumpers, blankets and rugs. Tourists can visit the factory to find out more about the traditional and modern production methods behind Icelandic knitwear.

**Sheep farming,
Northern Iceland**
Although an undoubtedly
picturesque industry, sheep
farming in Iceland has faced
many of the same challenges
as sheep farming elsewhere in
the world, with falling meat
prices and rising production
costs. Those who persist with
working sheep farms often
do so mainly out of loyalty
to the land and creatures
their families have tended
for decades.

BELOW:

Víðimýrarkirkja, Varmahlíð,
Built in 1834 (although housing bells that date back to 1630), the Víðimýrarkirkja church is the ultimate expression of ecclesiastical modesty – a simple turf-covered building, its basic frame made from driftwood collected from the shoreline of the Skagi Peninsula. The turf on the roof needs regular replacing as it dries out and becomes weathered.

RIGHT TOP:

Hofsós, Skagafjörður
Hofsós nestles on the eastern shore of the Skagafjörður fiord, a small habitation with a bigger past – formerly it was one of the most important trading posts in Iceland.

RIGHT BOTTOM:

Hofsós, Skagafjörður
Although a minor settlement (the population is fewer than 200), Hofsós is architecturally attractive and tranquil. Features for tourists and locals alike include a fjord-side swimming pool, the Iceland Emigration Centre museum and an annual Midsummer's Day festival.

OPPOSITE:

Laufás, Eyjafjörður
No form of architecture better represents the traditional way of Icelandic life than the turf house, of which Laufás has some of the finest examples. These buildings are preserved by the National Museum of Iceland. They are actually bigger than many turf houses of the past, because they were developed by a wealthy landowner.

LEFT:

Lake Mývatn, Northeast Iceland

Wreathed in mist, the silence broken only by the flock of geese flying overhead, Lake Mývatn is one of the jewels of northern Iceland. At 36.5 sq km (14 sq miles), it is Iceland's fourth-biggest lake. It is also referred to by some as the 'Northern Lights Capital of Iceland', the dark night skies giving perfect viewing conditions for the *aurora*.

ABOVE:

Heimskautsgerðið, Raufarhöfn

The Heimskautsgerðið, or Arctic Henge, stands as if a legacy of prehistory, but its construction actually began in 1996. The stones are specifically inspired by the 72 dwarves featured in an ancient eddic poem *Völuspá* (Prophecy of the Seeress), each dwarf connected to a specific seasonal element. Reaching up to 10m (32ft) in height, the stones evoke primordial feelings.

Akureyri, Northern Iceland
Akureyri is the second largest city in Iceland after Reykjavík, hence has attracted the name 'The Capital of North Iceland'. Although not a big city in terms of pure population size (18,000), Akureyri nevertheless has a vibrant social and cultural life, making it another must-see destination on the island.

Hof Cultural and Concert Centre, Akureyri

Opened in August 2010, the Hof Cultural and Concert Centre has in its short years become a prime destination for Icelandic musical, cultural and commercial events, with two large auditoriums and many other facilities. In sympathy with its location on the banks of a fjord, the building's exterior is formed primarily from rectangular blocks of Icelandic granite called Studlaberg.

ABOVE:

Icelandic Horses, Northern Iceland

While many people explore Iceland by car, on foot or by boat, for those wanting equestrian adventure, tours on the back of Icelandic horses are popular, as well as being ecologically friendly. The horses are known for their strength, endurance and their smooth-riding qualities.

OPPOSITE:

Icelandic Horses, Northern Iceland

Among those in the know, the Icelandic horses are respected for a specific type of gait, the *töltl*, defined as a four-beat gait that represents both walking and running, although the horse can perform it at a variety of different speeds to adjust for the nature of the terrain.

LEFT:

**Whale watching,
Northern Iceland**
A sight never to be forgotten.
Several tons of Humpback
whale breaches the Icelandic
coastal waters. In addition
to Humpbacks, Iceland's
seas are also home to Orcas,
Minke whales and the
mightiest creature on Earth,
the Blue whale.

OPPOSITE:

Goðafoss, Northeast Iceland
Another view of the great
Goðafoss waterfall, this
time under the heavenly
swirls of the *aurora borealis*.
According to legend,
when the lawgiver Þorgeir
(Thorgeir) Ljósvetningagoði
participated in his decision
to convert Iceland to
Christianity in 1000, he threw
his household pagan gods
into the waterfall.

Sauðárkrókur, Skagafjörður
A peaceful harbour scene at Sauðárkrókur. With a population of c. 2600, the town is one of the larger urban areas of North Iceland. Nature and culture are equal draws for visitors here, features including the nearby Grettislaug geothermal pool a little way out the town and iron workshops, music venues and excellent historical archives in the town.

OPPOSITE:

Húsavík, Skjálfandi Bay
A Humpback whale breaches in the Skjálfandi Bay near Húsavík, with the snow-laced Víknafjöll and Kinnarfjöll mountain ranges on the other side of the water. The bay waters are also home to dolphins, while the island of Lundey features an enormous colony of puffins.

ABOVE:

Húsavík, Skjálfandi Bay
The harbourside in Húsavík during the summer months forms a quaint and harmonious picture. The church standing a lofty 26m (85ft) high in the background, and acting as a visual anchor over the harbour, was built in 1907, and designed by the state architect, Rögnvaldur Ólafsson.

RIGHT:

Hverfjall, near Lake Mývatn
Superlatives struggle to describe the brute majesty of the Hverfjall, a 396m (1300ft) high volcanic crater. The crater, which is 1km (0.6 miles) in diameter, was formed from an earth-splitting eruption in 2300 BC; the magnitude of that event likely changed the atmosphere of the planet.

Hverarönd, Northern Iceland

A remote road navigates its way through the Hverarönd, a geologically active region known for its hot springs, fumaroles, and boiling (literally) mud pools. Also known as Námaskarð, the area has a distinct sulphurous smell in the air, and visitors must take guided care to avoid burns and inhalation injuries from the heated landscape.

Dettifoss, Vatnajökull National Park

The Dettifoss waterfall thunders its voice into the basin of the Jökulsárgljúfur canyon. While some of Iceland's waterfalls draw attention with their beauty, Dettifoss compels with its power. It is 100m (328ft) wide and has a drop of 44m (144ft), with the largest volume discharge of water of any waterfall in the country, and indeed in Europe.

RIGHT:

Siglufjörður, Fjallabyggð

The small fishing village of Siglufjörður built itself upon the herring fishing industry, which took the town to a population of 3000 in the mid-20th century. That industry has since disappeared, and the population has dropped to 1200, but the pretty town still remembers its past in the large and impressive Herring Era Museum.

OPPOSITE TOP LEFT:

Icelandic herring

Herring with boiled potatoes – a classic Icelandic dish. In the herring industry's heyday, the fish accounted for between 25 and 45 per cent of Iceland's entire exports income.

OPPOSITE BOTTOM LEFT:

Siglufjörður, Fjallabyggð

Another view of Siglufjörður. Although the herring industry has gone from northern Iceland, the town has rejuvenated, and today warrants a visit by travellers wanting a combination of charm and access to the surrounding wilderness.

OPPOSITE TOP RIGHT:

Grimsey Island

Freshly caught Atlantic Rose fish are packed in ice on Grimsey Island.

OPPOSITE BOTTOM RIGHT:

Mývatn, Northeast Iceland

Salmon fish being smoked in the traditional manner.

Volcanic landscape, Northern Iceland

Apart from the road cutting across its surface, this volcanic landscape near Mývatn speaks more of prehistory than modernity. Iceland has a very high concentration of active volcanoes – 30 systems in total – on account of its placement on the Mid-Atlantic Ridge (MAR) tectonic plate boundary.

ABOVE:
Holuhraun, Highlands, Northeastern Iceland
The Holuhraun is a lava field just north of the Vatnajökull ice cap, located above the Bárðarbunga and Askja volcano systems. As these photographs indicate, it is highly active, the landscape changing with each new eruption. The last great eruption was in August 2014–February 2015, a seventh-month event that created a lava field 85 sq km (33 sq miles).

RIGHT:
Holuhraun, Highlands, Northeastern Iceland
The 2014–15 eruption of the Holuhraun totally eclipsed the previous eruption (in the 18th century) in size and scale. Thankfully, there were no human fatalities from the event, although some communities were told to stay indoors for periods to avoid toxic gases. There have been many sheep deaths from poisoned grasslands, however.

RIGHT AND OPPOSITE:

Námafjall Geothermal Area, Northeastern Iceland

Mudpots and mud pools abound in the Námafjall Geothermal Area, located to the east of Lake Mývatn. Sulphur gas, pushing its way through glutinous mud, create these bubbling pits, plus a variety of other geological phenomena, including gas vents and steam springs. Because of the chemical conditions surrounding the geothermal activity, almost no vegetation survives in the Námafjall. The area also includes the power plant that taps into the physical conditions, and produces 3MW of geothermal energy every year.

Eastern Region

Iceland has such a plethora and concentration of natural wonders that it is a futile task to attempt to place them in any sort of ranking. Yet the Eastern Region, on the opposite side of the island from the tourist magnet that is Reykjavík, has some justifiable contenders. Chief of all would arguably be the Vatnajökull glacier, from which some 30 other outlet glaciers take their source. An engulfing landscape of ice, frozen to the naked eye but in reality moving with infinite patience, it still shapes the terrain and the climate, the ice rivers and plates being a seminal part of a greater whole, the Vatnajökull National Park.

In some ways, it is the ice that speaks of the future of Iceland. For as the wider world grows warmer, Iceland does so too, its northerly location proving no barrier against global climatic effects. As the degrees on the thermometer steadily inch upwards, and the Icelandic winters appear to become shorter, so to does the ice retreat year on year. Long term, and assuming that the changes are largely irreversible, how this will change the life and ecology of Iceland is open to question. Yet regardless of change, Eastern Iceland continues to overawe its inhabitants and visitors with a landscape that, once seen, cannot be forgotten.

OPPOSITE:
Borgarfjörður Eystri, Eastern Iceland
Those from Eastern Iceland exhibit the same resilience and pioneering spirit as the rest of Iceland's inhibitants. The village of Borgarfjörður Eystri has only 100 inhabitants, the low-rise buildings dwarfed by the mountainous background and the blue lofted vault of the Icelandic skies.

Diamond Beach, Jökulsárlón Glacial Lagoon
The thinking behind the 'Diamond Beach' title is evident here, as the low sun turns shoreside blocks of ice into glowing, glass-like objects. The ice comes from the Breiðamerkurjökull glacier, and many of the blocks of ice that break off have been in their frozen form for hundreds of years.

**Svartifoss Waterfall,
Skaftafell**

Appearing like the set of a
fantasy movie, the Svartifoss
(Black Falls) waterfall takes
its name from the horseshoe
of basalt cliffs that stack up
like organ pipes around the
water, which drops 20m (66ft)
from the top.

OPPOSITE:

**Jökulsárlón, Southeast
Iceland**

The Jökulsárlón glacier
lagoon is choked with ice,
the ice flowing in from the
Vatnajökull, one of Europe's
largest glaciers, just to the
north. The blocks of ice
range in size from minor ice
balls up to full-blown icebergs
the size of a building.

OPPOSITE:

Ice patterns, East Iceland
The ice that masses in the seas and lakes of Iceland is hewn into fantastical shapes by the sea, wind and rain. Here a near-symmetrical passageway has been cut through a sheer wall of ice. The clear blue colour of the ice indicates that it has a glacial origin.

RIGHT:

Jökulsárlón, Southeast Iceland
Ice melts as it calves from the Jökulsárlón glacier and heads out to sea. The smooth and glass-like surface of this piece of ice is due to the wind and sea spray buffing out the hard edges.

ABOVE:

Jökulsárlón, Southeast Iceland
Ice rolls in on the surf at the Black Beach, another name for
the aforementioned Diamond Beach. The lake is part of the
Vatnajökull National Park, a vast natural region that covers
much of central Iceland.

RIGHT:

Jökulsárlón, Southeast Iceland
A haunting night-time vision of the Jökulsárlón glacier lagoon.
A photograph cannot provide the strange auditory signatures
of the lagoon, with the ice creaking and cracking as the blocks
rub together in the water.

LEFT AND BELOW LEFT:

Icelandic foods

The traditional foods of the Icelandic people are, to many modern palates, rather austere, although they are nutritious and wholesome. At the top we here see some *harðfiskur* (dried fish) and black bread. Icelandic breads (below left) are diverse in type. One of the most traditional is *rúgbrauð*, a rye bread baked in a pot or wooden cask by burying the vessel in the ground near a hot spring.

RIGHT:

East Iceland

Long strips of the Eastern Iceland coastline are nearly devoid of human habitation, or have thinly spread populations. Here an isolated house appears to be perilously close to the shoreline.

Eskifjörður, Eastern Fjords

Eskifjörður is in the Eastern Fjords, specifically on the edge of the Eskifjörður fjord, a northern arm of Reyðarfjörður fjord. Here an enterprising local has turned a small boat into a hot tub, with views of the mountains in the background; the Eskja and Hólmatindur mountains are the main geological features overlooking the fjord.

OPPOSITE:

Eskifjörður, Eastern Fjords

Eskifjörður has a population of just over 1000 people. Commercially, the town is focused upon fishing and fish processing, industries that it has pursued since the 1700s. Eskifjörður was also one of the first towns in Iceland to derive its domestic heating water from geothermal sources.

LEFT:

Höfn, Hornafjörður

Fishing vessels sits on water of glass-like smoothness during a misty morning at Höfn. The town is known for its excellent offshore fishing, including for species such as Norwegian lobster (*Nephrops norvegicus*), caught from few other ports in Iceland.

OPPOSITE:

Klifbrekkufossar, Mjóifjörður

Tumbling down the mountainside in a series of small steps, the sparkling Klifbrekkufossar waterfalls are fed from springs flowing out from the Mjóafjarðarheiði heath. Because of its spring source, the water is exceptionally pure in quality.

Vestrahorn/Brunnhorn Mountains, Hvalnes Peninsula
The Vestrahorn Mountain, to the left of the picture here, and the neighbouring Brunnhorn Mountain, are two of an impressive sequence of mountains on the Hvalnes Peninsula. The Brunnhorn Mountain is also known among locals as the 'Batman Mountain', on account of the perceived resemblance between the mountain's shape and the eponymous superhero's logo.

ABOVE:

Vestrahorn/Brunnhorn Mountains, Hvalnes Peninsula
The Vestrahorn Mountain is one of the most photographed mountains in Iceland. Its impact is enhanced by the black sand and mud landscape that surrounds it, contrasting beautifully with the snow on the peaks and the endless sky above.

RIGHT:

Skaftafellsjökull Glacier, Öræfi
The Skaftafellsjökull glacier demonstrates perfectly how ice plus time are able to carve out entire valleys and mountains. Although visually compelling, the area can be dangerous for unguided people; the surrounding landscape is prone to lethal and sudden landslides.

Skaftafellsjökull Glacier, Öræfi

Another view along the Skaftafellsjökull glacier, humbling the viewer with its scale. The glacier measures a mighty 10km (6 miles) long and 2km (1.2 miles) wide, the glacial ice cut through with chasms and fissures, and carrying rocks and debris with it. The ice flows down the valley from the north part of the nearby Öræfajökull glacier.

OPPOSITE:

Vatnajökull Glacier, Vatnajökull National Park
The Vatnajökull glacier is vast in scale – it covers an area of
8100 sq. km (3127 sq. miles) and in places the ice is 1km (0.6
miles) deep; the average thickness of the ice is 400m (1312ft).
Some 30 outlet glaciers run off the Vatnajökull, including the
aforementioned Skaftafellsjökull

ABOVE:

Vatnajökull Glacier, Vatnajökull National Park
Designated in 2008, the Vatnajökull National Park covers
approximately 14 per cent of Iceland's landmass, and it
includes Iceland's highest mountain – Hvannadalshjúkur –
which towers over the surrounding region at 2109m (6921ft) in
elevation. This photo perfectly evokes the region's isolation.

LEFT:

Heinabergsfljot River, Eastern Iceland

An ominous sign of the future? Glacial melting has rendered this old iron bridge over the Heinabergsfljot River redundant. Iceland's glaciers and ice caps are retreating at a record rate. Some of the islanders see this as an ecological disaster, while others reflect on possible benefits to trade and transport.

ABOVE:

Skaftafell National Park, Eastern Iceland

The Skaftafell National Park was established in 1967, and in 2008 it became part of the far larger Vatnajökull National Park. Nestled amid the rugged scenery are occasional signs of former habitation, including these old turf houses, which the landscape seems intent on absorbing.

LEFT:

Vatnajökull Glacier, Vatnajökull National Park
The interior of an ice cave in the Vatnajökull glacier is a magical sight to behold. The ice, maybe 1000 years old, has lost all impurities (hence its spectral clarity) and has been compressed into a steel-like hardness.

OPPOSITE:

Svínafellsjökull Glacier, Vatnajökull National Park
The Svínafellsjökull is actually a 'glacial tongue', extending out from the mighty Vatnajökull ice cap. A cultural point of note is that Svínafellsjökull was used in the TV drama *Game of Thrones* to represent the bleak 'north side of the Wall'.

Picture Credits